D1561201

Space

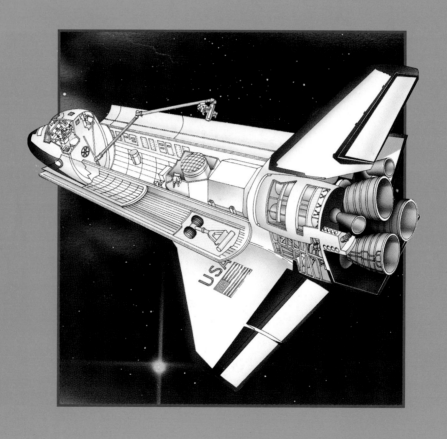

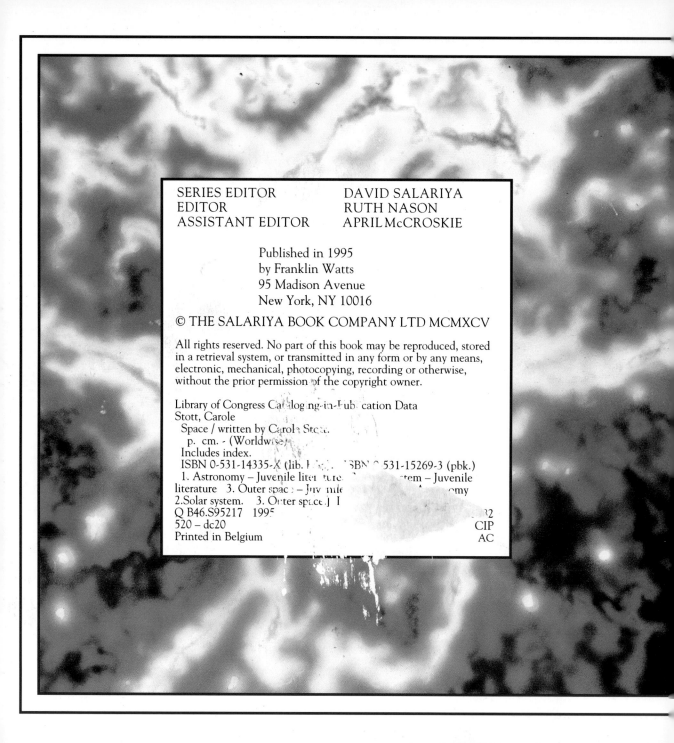

SERIES EDITOR   DAVID SALARIYA
EDITOR   RUTH NASON
ASSISTANT EDITOR   APRIL McCROSKIE

Published in 1995
by Franklin Watts
95 Madison Avenue
New York, NY 10016

© THE SALARIYA BOOK COMPANY LTD MCMXCV

Library of Congress Cataloging-in-Publication Data
Stott, Carole
  Space / written by Carole Stott.
    p. cm. - (Worldwise)
  Includes index.
  ISBN 0-531-14335-X (lib. bdg.). ISBN 0-531-15269-3 (pbk.)
    1. Astronomy – Juvenile literature.   tem – Juvenile
literature 3. Outer space – Juvenile   omy
2.Solar system.   3. Outer space.] I
Q B46.S95217 1995   82
520 – dc20   CIP
Printed in Belgium   AC

worldwise
Space

Written by
CAROLE STOTT
Illustrated by
SIMON CALDER & LEE PETERS

Series created & designed by
DAVID SALARIYA

WATTS BOOKS

CONTENTS

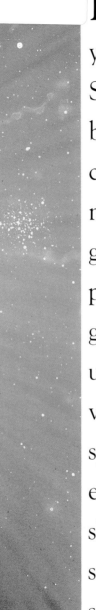

Look up into the sky and you are looking into space. The Sun lights up Earth's daytime sky, but it limits the view. At night you can see thousands of objects from millions of miles away. At such great distances the stars look like pinpoints of light, and even whole galaxies are only bright smudges to us on Earth. Close-up the view is very different. Space is full of giant spinning balls of glowing gas and exploding stars. Space has potato-shaped moons, city-sized dirty snowballs that are too small to be seen from Earth, and much more.

*You and millions of
other forms of life
live in the Universe.*

*Earth is your home.
It is a big ball of rock,
almost covered
by water and
surrounded by gas.*

Earth is one of
nine planets that
orbit the Sun.
Together they are
the Solar System.

The Sun is a star.
It is one of at least
100 billion stars
that make the
spiral-shaped Milky
Way galaxy.

The Universe is everything – everything you can see, everything you can think of, and much, much more. The Universe contains you and your home, the planet Earth. It includes the Solar System, which is Earth's family, and the Milky Way galaxy, the massive star system in which we live. At vast distances are many millions more galaxies, each one moving away from the others. The Universe is getting bigger all the time.

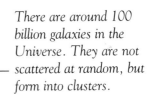

There are around 100 billion galaxies in the Universe. They are not scattered at random, but form into clusters.

The Sun is a star – a hot spinning ball of luminous gas. It is the biggest object in the Solar System. Some 110 Earths would fit across its face.

Enormous flares of glowing gas called prominences shoot out from the Sun's surface. They can stretch hundreds of thousands of miles into space. Sunspots are cool, dark spots on the Sun's surface, but even these are more than 8,000° F (4,000° C).

The Sun is made mainly of hydrogen gas that it converts to helium at the rate of more than 600 million tons every second. As it works, it produces lots of heat and light in its core. At 59 million degrees fahrenheit (15 million degrees centigrade), the core is the Sun's hottest part.

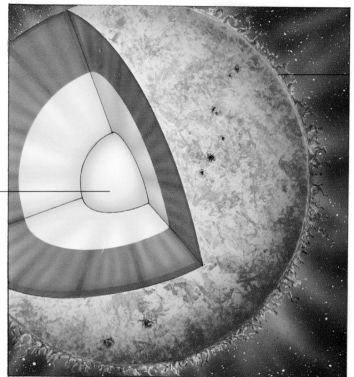

Earth is just far enough away from the Sun for life to survive. If our planet was much closer it would be too hot. Much farther away and it would be too cold.

The planets close to the Sun are the hottest and the brightest. The more distant ones hardly feel the Sun's heat and see the Sun only as a bright star in the sky.

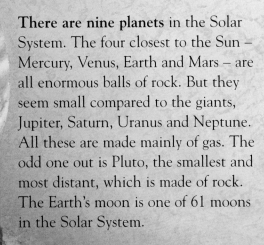

10

9

8

7

6

There are nine planets in the Solar System. The four closest to the Sun – Mercury, Venus, Earth and Mars – are all enormous balls of rock. But they seem small compared to the giants, Jupiter, Saturn, Uranus and Neptune. All these are made mainly of gas. The odd one out is Pluto, the smallest and most distant, which is made of rock. The Earth's moon is one of 61 moons in the Solar System.

1. Pluto	6.	Neptune
2. Mercury	7.	Uranus
3. Mars	8.	Saturn
4. Venus	9.	Jupiter
5. Earth	10.	Sun

5

4

3

2

1

The Sun and its family

are called the Solar System. Around 4.6 billion years ago material in a gas and dust cloud formed the Sun. The leftovers made the planets and their moons, as well as comets and asteroids. The Sun's gravity keeps its family together in space.

Gases form Earth's atmosphere, which keeps just the right amount of heat in at the surface to support life.

Ancestors of today's marine life appeared 3.5 billion years ago. Shellfish appeared about 500 million years ago.

Land plants and animals with back-bones didn't appear until about 400 million years ago. Dinosaurs lived from about 200 to 64 million years ago.

Humans started to evolve about 4 million years ago.

Satellites in orbit around Earth can look down and collect information about our weather system. They identify mineral deposits, crops and movements of sea life.

Earth is unique.

It is the only planet we know of with water and life. Around three quarters of its surface is covered in water, and millions of different life forms live on Earth. Spacecraft landed on nearby Mars in 1976 and equipment on board tested for signs of life. But Mars is a lifeless world, even though it has the ingredients to form life.

Mars is about half the size of Earth and much colder.

Mars has volcanoes, mountains, deserts and canyons all bigger than those on Earth. The volcano Olympus Mons is three times as high as the highest mountain on Earth.

The red color of Mars comes from the red rock and dust covering its surface. Specks of dust float around it and so Mars has a pink sky.

At least 16 moons travel with Jupiter as it orbits the Sun. Ganymede and Io and two others are larger than the planet Pluto.

The Galileo space probe will have reached Jupiter in December 1995.

Jupiter is the biggest

planet. If all the other eight planets were put together, they would equal only a third of Jupiter. It is made mainly of hydrogen gas with liquid and a small rocky core. From Earth it looks like a silver-bright star in the sky. By looking through telescopes we can see its banded surface and some of its moons. But the most stunning images of Jupiter, so far, have come from spacecraft that have visited it.

Cloud tops form into dark bands and bright zones. The twisty patterns in the bands are caused by winds moving the gas around. Jupiter's main gas is hydrogen, with some helium.

Jupiter's ring was discovered in January 1979. The spacecraft Voyager 1 gave us our first view of it. It is invisible from Earth.

The Great Red Spot is one of a number of giant storms on Jupiter. This is the biggest storm in the Solar System. At least two Earths could fit inside it.

A day on Jupiter lasts only ten hours. Jupiter is the fastest spinning planet. Its fast spin produces high-speed winds and storms and makes its center bulge out.

Saturn's clouds form
bands around the planet.

Two identical space probes, Voyager 1 and 2, flew by Saturn, one in 1980 and the next in 1981. Several new moons were discovered, and we got our first detailed look at Saturn's rings.

Voyager's instruments investigated
Saturn, its rings and moons, and
cameras took thousands of images. All
the information was sent back to Earth by
the 13-foot (4 m) bowl-shaped antenna.

18

All four gas giants - Jupiter, Saturn, Uranus and Neptune - have rings, but Saturn's are the most memorable. They are made of millions of chunks of icy rock, ranging in size from grains of sand to elephant-sized boulders.

Saturn has at least 18 moons. The largest, Titan, is unusual. It is the only moon in the Solar System with a thick atmosphere. The smallest moons are only a few miles across.

Saturn looks like a star in Earth's sky. Space probe images have shown us what a stunning planet this is close-up. Like Jupiter, Saturn is made mainly of hydrogen and helium gas. Storms have been seen, and winds up to 1,120 mph (1,800 kph) have been measured. On pages 16 and 17 a comet collides with Jupiter.

— *Ariel*

Scientists already knew of five Uranian moons, including Ariel, before Voyager 2 discovered more. Neptune's moon total became eight.

Dark and white spots travel around Neptune (left). The Great Dark Spot is a huge storm. The white spots are clouds of methane ice. One travels around every 17 hours and is nicknamed "the scooter."

Uranus spins on its side as it travels around the Sun. Its system of moons and its rings go around its center. Both Uranus and Neptune are made chiefly of hydrogen and helium gas. A third gas, methane, gives the planets their color.

Uranus and Neptune

were almost unknown worlds to us until the Voyager 2 spacecraft visited them. It flew by Uranus first, in 1986. Three and a half years later, it reached Neptune. Even close-up Uranus is a featureless globe, but Neptune has some bands and white clouds around it.

Sixteen new moons were discovered, ten for Uranus and six for Neptune.

— *Uranus*

21

Earth

Sun

Mercury

Venus

Mercury and Venus are the closest

planets to the Sun. They are both
made of rock but are different worlds.
Mercury looks like Earth's moon, covered in
craters. We cannot see the surface of Venus.
It is blanketed by a poisonous atmosphere.
But the clouds at the top of the atmosphere
reflect sunlight and make Venus easy to see
in Earth's nighttime sky.

Pluto is the farthest planet from the Sun. It is a frozen, dark world.

Heat from the Sun penetrates Venus's clouds and warms up the surface. The clouds then trap the heat.

Underneath Venus's clouds is a rocky surface with mountains, lowlands and rolling plains.

Mercury has almost no atmosphere. In the daytime the planet is burning hot at 750° F (400° C). But with no atmosphere to keep the heat in, Mercury's nights are freezing cold at -325° F (-200° C).

The Caloris Basin is a gigantic crater on Mercury's surface. It is some 800 miles (1,300km) in diameter – about the length of the California coastline.

A space probe called Mariner 10 gave us most of our information about Mercury. In 1974 it took photographs of one whole side of it.

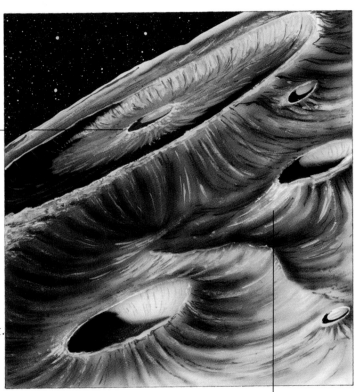

A year on Mercury lasts only 88 days; that's how long the planet takes to make one complete orbit around the Sun. But the planet spins around slowly. It takes nearly 59 Earth days to spin around once.

Mariner 10

Mercury's craters were formed when rocks crashed into the young planet some 4 billion years ago at a time of possible volcanic activity.

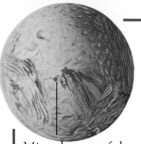

Miranda, one of the moons of Uranus, has a surface with a strange mixture of craters, canyons, and cliffs. Scientists believe that it has experienced upheaval in the past.

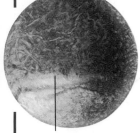

Triton, one of Neptune's moons, is a bright, icy moon. In 1989, Voyager 2 recorded surface details half a mile (1 km) across.

On pages 24-25 is a moon landing. Twelve men have walked on Earth's moon. They brought back over 880 pounds (400 kg) of rock and crossed 56 miles (90 km) of its surface.

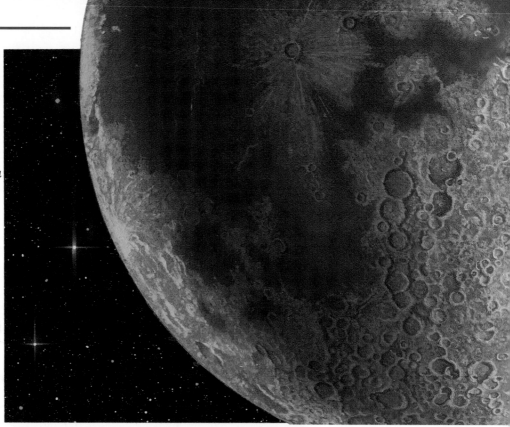

The same side of our moon always faces us on Earth. The dark areas are lower land, the brighter areas, higher land. We did not know what the other side of the moon looked like until a spacecraft took photographs in 1959.

Callisto is one of Jupiter's, and one of the Solar System's, biggest moons. Its craters formed when space rocks bombarded it.

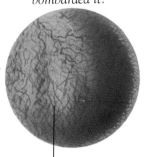

Europa is a smooth-surfaced moon that travels around Jupiter every three and a half days. It is a little smaller than our moon but much colder.

The sixty-one known moons in the Solar System are rocky and icy bodies. Each moon travels around its own planet, and all planets and moons travel around the Sun. All the planets except Mercury and Venus have moons. Saturn has the most moons.

Gaspra

Asteroids are mini rocky bodies that travel around the Sun. There are millions of them. Gaspra is about 7.5 miles (12 km) across.

Most comets stay at the edge of the Solar System. A few, called periodic comets, travel around the Sun, repeating the journey after a set period of time.

Way beyond Pluto there are billions of comets. Each one is a large dirty snowball made of snow and dust. If a comet travels close to the Sun, it produces gas and dust tails millions of miles long.

When the Solar System was born the Sun was formed first. It used up the biggest share of the cloud of gas and dust. Next came the planets and their moons. What was left made the asteroids and the comets. Most asteroids are found in the asteroid belt, a ring of rocks between Mars and Jupiter. Comets are found at the very edge of the Solar System.

We live with the Sun in the Milky Way galaxy. There are at least 100 billion more stars there. The stars form a spiral, and we live in one of its arms, about two thirds of the way from the center.

There are four main types of galaxy: spiral, barred spiral, elliptical and irregular.

The stars you see in Earth's night sky belong to the Milky Way galaxy. From Earth we can look either out toward its edge, or, for those in the southern hemisphere, into its center. The path of milky light from millions of stars gave the Milky Way galaxy its name.

Earth's moon

The Milky Way

Shooting stars

Elliptical galaxies contain old stars and are the most common type of galaxy. They can be egg-shaped, ball-shaped or squashed-ball shaped.

A spiral galaxy is a disk-shaped family of stars where arms of stars come out from the center. Spiral galaxies are made of young and old stars. If the arms come from a bar of stars at the galaxy's center, the galaxy is a barred spiral.

Irregular galaxies are those where the stars have not formed into any regular shape. These are the rarest of all galaxies.

Galaxies are collections of millions of stars, and there are around 100 billion galaxies in the Universe. All galaxies started their lives as a giant cloud of spinning gas. As the cloud spun, stars formed and the galaxy took shape. Those that spun the fastest became the flattest galaxies.

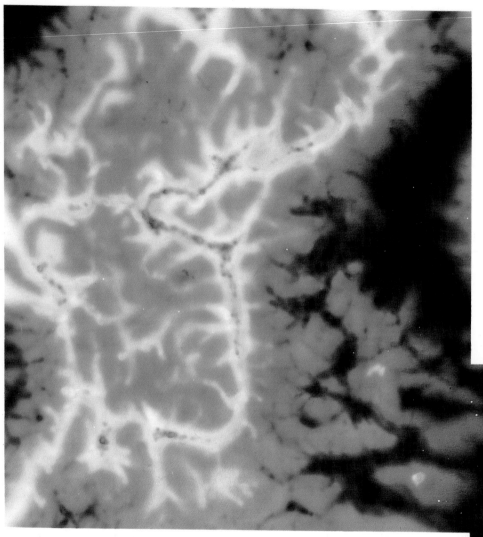

Stars change as they get older. In about 5 billion years the Sun will expand and turn red to become a red giant.

Stars are made of two main gases, hydrogen and helium.

All stars are born in the same way. How they live and die depends on how much gas they are made of.

A supernova is a star that dies by blowing itself apart. From Earth the star looks like a very bright star in the sky.

Material from a supernova can form a nebula and eventually be used to produce new stars.

Red giant

White dwarf

Black dwarf

Eventually, the Sun will become a white dwarf, then slowy fade to become a black dwarf.

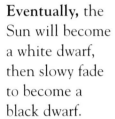

There are more stars in the Universe than anything else. There are so many that you couldn't count them in your lifetime. From Earth they look like sparkling pinpoints of light in the night sky. But, close up, they are massive spinning balls of hot, glowing gas. Stars are born from clouds of gas and dust. They grow older and, after a lifetime lasting millions or billions of years, they die.

The cloud of gas and dust where a star is born is called a nebula. Mini clouds of material form inside it and become dense and hot. These are called protostars. As a protostar gets hotter, it starts to shine and a star is born.

The first humans looked

into the night sky and out into space. They just used their eyes to see hundreds of stars. They called some the wandering stars, and these we know as the planets. Today we use computer-controlled telescopes, high on mountaintops, away from city lights and above the clouds, to look into space and record what they see for us.

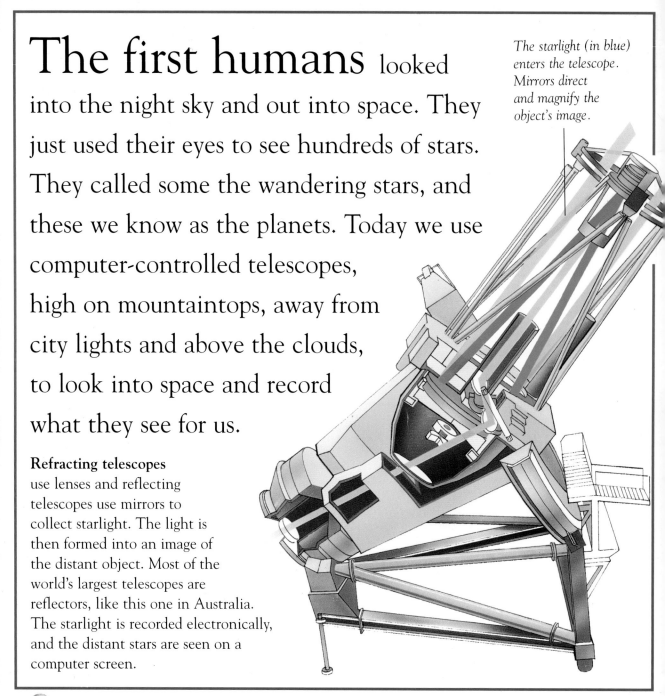

The starlight (in blue) enters the telescope. Mirrors direct and magnify the object's image.

Refracting telescopes use lenses and reflecting telescopes use mirrors to collect starlight. The light is then formed into an image of the distant object. Most of the world's largest telescopes are reflectors, like this one in Australia. The starlight is recorded electronically, and the distant stars are seen on a computer screen.

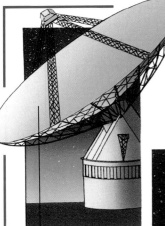

Earth-based telescopes look and listen into space, since most light and radio waves get through Earth's atmosphere. Satellite telescopes can give us other views.

Satellite dishes back on Earth collect information signals from the telescopes in space, in much the same way as smaller satellite dishes on houses collect television signals.

Earth's atmosphere protects us. It stops most of the Sun's harmful ultraviolet rays from reaching us and burning our skin. But it also stops other waves that astronomers want to collect. So astronomers put their telescopes into orbit above Earth's atmosphere to collect as much information as they can from space.

From 310 miles (500 km) above Earth, this satellite collects light and ultraviolet waves from space.

An infrared satellite telescope shows us where the hot or cold places are in the Universe.

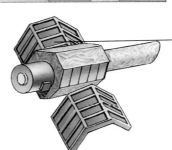

It takes 8 minutes only for this ultraviolet satellite to send information down to Earth.

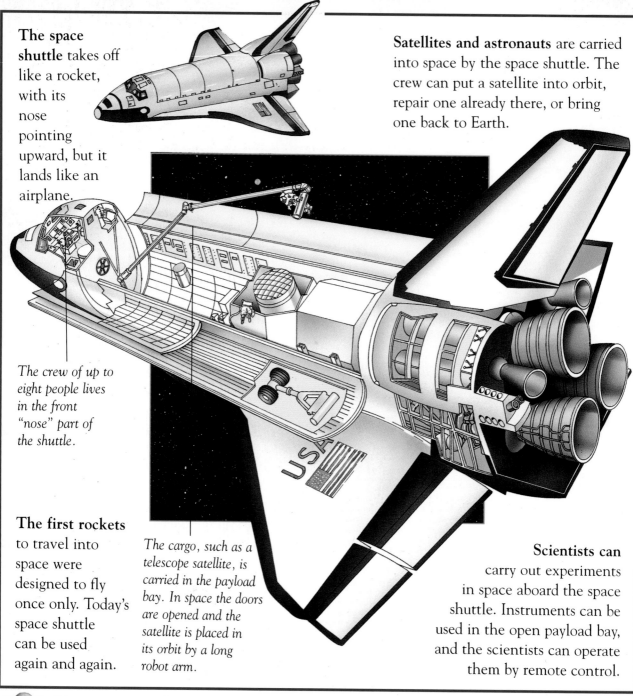

The space shuttle takes off like a rocket, with its nose pointing upward, but it lands like an airplane.

Satellites and astronauts are carried into space by the space shuttle. The crew can put a satellite into orbit, repair one already there, or bring one back to Earth.

The crew of up to eight people lives in the front "nose" part of the shuttle.

The first rockets to travel into space were designed to fly once only. Today's space shuttle can be used again and again.

The cargo, such as a telescope satellite, is carried in the payload bay. In space the doors are opened and the satellite is placed in its orbit by a long robot arm.

Scientists can carry out experiments in space aboard the space shuttle. Instruments can be used in the open payload bay, and the scientists can operate them by remote control.

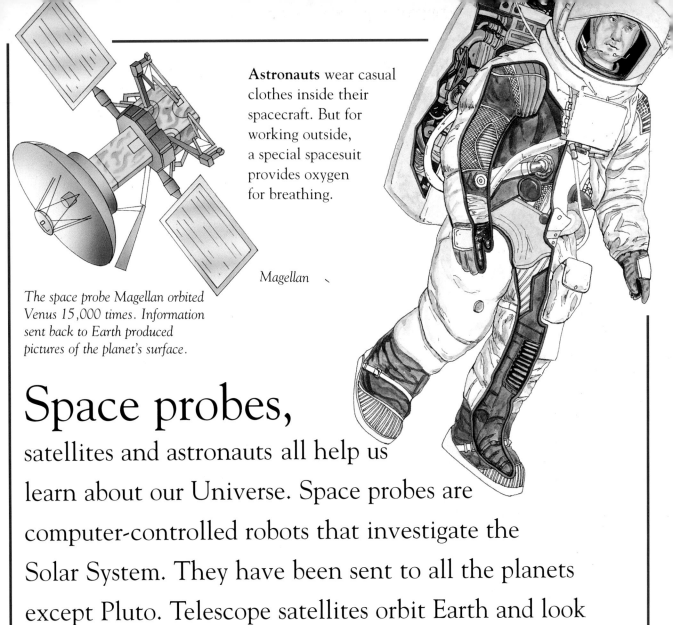

Astronauts wear casual clothes inside their spacecraft. But for working outside, a special spacesuit provides oxygen for breathing.

Magellan

The space probe Magellan orbited Venus 15,000 times. Information sent back to Earth produced pictures of the planet's surface.

Space probes,

satellites and astronauts all help us learn about our Universe. Space probes are computer-controlled robots that investigate the Solar System. They have been sent to all the planets except Pluto. Telescope satellites orbit Earth and look out into space. Astronauts have visited the moon and traveled and worked in space near Earth.

USEFUL WORDS

Asteroid A small rocky body orbiting the Sun.

Atmosphere The layer of gas surrounding a planet or moon.

Billion One million million or 1 with twelve zeros after it.

Comet A half mile-sized ball of snow and dust that produces a head and tails if it travels close to the Sun.

Crater A round hollow on the surface of a planet or moon.

Gravity A pulling force that holds everything together; stars in a galaxy, planets around a star, and objects on Earth.

Million 1,000,000

Moon A rocky body orbiting a planet.

Orbit The path a planet or comet takes around the Sun, and the path a moon takes around a planet.

Planet A body of rock, or rock and gas, orbiting a star.

Red giant An old large and bright star.

Satellite A man-made instrument like a telescope that orbits the Earth, or a moon orbiting a planet.

Space rock A lump of rock that has broken off from a planet or an asteroid.

Star A spinning ball of hot and luminous gas.

White dwarf A dim, small star at the end of its life.

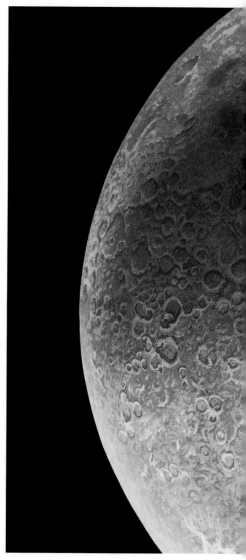

INDEX

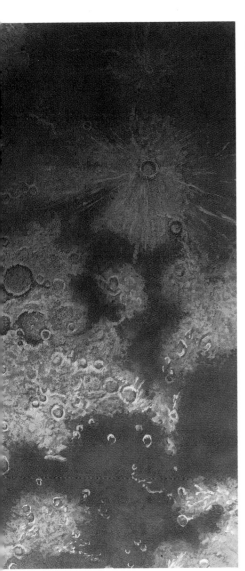